When you need a CHANGE

Dr. D. K. Olukoya

When you NEED A CHANGE

Dr. D.K Olukoya

WHEN YOU NEED A CHANGE
© 2011 DR. D. K. OLUKOYA
ISBN 978-978-8424-62-8
January 2011

Published by:
Mountain of Fire and Miracles Ministries Press
13, Olasimbo Street, Onike, Yaba, Lagos.

I salute my wonderful wife, Pastor Shade, for her invaluable support in the ministry.
I appreciate her unquantifiable support in the book ministry as the cover designer, art editor and art adviser

All Scripture quotation is from the King James Version of the Bible

All rights reserved.
We prohibit reproduction in whole or part without written permission

CONTENTS	Pages
WHEN YOU NEED A CHANGE	5
THE STRANGE ACTS OF GOD	10
THE TRUTH YOU CANNOT AVOID	18
WOLVES, SERPENTS, SCORPIONS	27
THE BAPTISM OF THE HOLY SPIRIT	32
AN UNFORGETTABLE ENCOUNTER	37

CHAPTER ONE

WHEN YOU
need a
CHANGE

Change is, actually, the very essence of life itself, and when, a person resists change, the person is working against life. There are some changes, that one may be required to make, which he, or she is not even ready to embrace. A lot of people would rather stick to their familiar past. A lot of people are afraid of going into unravelled territories, or taking any risk.

Many, stubbornly, cling to their ideas and habits. The Lord does not allow that. The nature of God's work includes changing, you must sincerely change. Read your Bible very well, and you will find out that men and women in the Scriptures, who moved mountain for the Lord, travelled in unknown territories. Moses did not see a previous example anywhere, but he did something, and the Red Sea parted. He took a holy risk, and God backed him up. However, you have to make a decision now to make a change.

Some friends may have to go, some ideas might have to be dropped and some habits might have to be changed, if you want the fullness of God in your life. You must make that decision to change. You must examine all your old habits and practices. You must examine all your old friends, and challenge all those traditions you have been following, which have yielded nothing.

In spite of the fact that, God is even trying to bring some people out of these traditions, their hearts, and spirits are still there, and

Jesus is, still, looking at them, asking "Can I really use this one?" So, you must challenge these things, you have been doing.

CHANGE AND ADVANCEMENT

Anybody, who would like to work with Jesus, must be prepared to change. Somebody, who was a drunk, suddenly, gives his life to the Lord, and becomes a new person. When you say, "Sir, were you not the one drinking in that place?" He would say, "That was before, I have now changed."

There is an expressway to the top. If you follow this pathway, you will experience an uncommon lift. Until you make certain changes, you will not be able to rise to the highest heights. When you change, you shall rise. Let me make it clear again, when you change, you rise.

> *"Moab hath been at ease from his youth, and he hath settled on his lees, and hath not been emptied from vessel to vessel, neither hath he gone into captivity: therefore his taste remained in him, and his scent is not changed." Jeremiah 48:11:*

God has designed this book, for some specific people. Here, we see that Moab had problems. He was used to a life of ease. He was settled on his lees. He was not emptied from vessel to vessel. He had not, really, tasted, what is called captivity, and because of that, his taste remained unaltered, and his flavour was not changed. The long and short of the matter concerning Moab, was that, he refused to change, and because of that, he stank.

MOVING BEHIND

Many of us are moving behind schedule. Some are meant to have helped thousands of people, but they are still busy, picking marbles in the street. Sometime ago, a couple came to see me, because they were fighting. I asked: "What was the matter?" The husband said, "Dr., tell this woman to be submissive," and I said, "Madam, why are you not submissive?" And, she said, "Excuse me, man of God, this submission, what is the meaning?" I counselled them and after sometime, I said, "Let us pray."

When I prayed, I was amazed at the revelation I got. I saw this couple standing on the top of a very tall building, with a long queue of people in their front, and the couple was distributing money to these people. These people were very grateful, thanking God for their lives. But, as they were distributing the money, I saw some naked women at their back, firing arrows at them. I said, "You people are busy fighting, instead of doing what God wants you to do." A change is necessary.

You must question those customs, that have not got you, anywhere. Somebody told me, he had been going to church for forty years, and when I asked him, if he has received the baptism of the Holy Spirit, he said, "How much do they sell it?" After giving him a lecture, he gave me a sum of two thousand naira. thanking him, I used the money to buy some books, that would help him, before he left.

A NEW ERA

This is a new era, and we must change for the best. Remember, a seed does not take root, unless it falls to the ground, and dies there. It will, then, change to something else, and begin to grow.

The seed would first of all look ugly. You begin to wonder why life is so unkind to it, as to break it in the middle. But, the truth is that, it has to change, before it brings out something.

The stars you see in the sky, do not shine much until it is very dark. Anybody, who is saying, "I am always what I was," is to be pitied. I mean the person is not ready for progress, and a person, who never changes, is a fool. It is stagnant water, that breeds mosquitoes. The law of change is so powerful, that you must comply with it. Sometimes, the problem with those who refuse to change, is that they love themselves more than the truth. So, if you love yourself more than the truth, deceive yourself for a while, then, things will start to happen.

RESULTS OF DELIVERANCE

Some brethren and I, ministered to a sister, who had a lot of problems. She read medicine, but it was as, if she did not go to school. She was married with four children. Her husband woke up one morning and said, "I don't know why, but I hate you, and I am leaving." The woman thought it was a joke, but the man packed his things and left. I asked her, if she was a Christian and she said, "yes", and described her church to me.

The first day she attended our service, I saw her and asked, "How was the service today?" She said, "Strange." I asked her what was strange about it, and she said, "In the church I used to attend, we danced for 4 hours, from 9 am - 1 pm. Sometimes, when you get home, your waist would be paining you, because of dancing." Anyway, she kept coming.

I asked her to go for deliverance, and she did. I saw her again and asked her how she was getting on, and she said, "Fine, but tough." "What is tough?" I demanded to know; "You see, see said, I had to remove my attachment, and discarded my jewellery. I am looking ugly now". It was hard for her to change, but when she began to follow the necessary directions, things began to happen.

MIRACLES GALORE

The first miracle she received was that, the British Nationality that had been denied her, in the past, was given to her after three weeks of her coming. She was pleasantly surprised. Immediately, her husband heard that she got the British Nationality, he came back and said, "Well, I just came to congratulate you." Then, she said, "Go now." He said, "No. I am staying here." That was how her marriage was restored.

When you change, things happen. We do a lot of spiritual warfare here. Eventually, everybody will get involved. There is no other way, because the dark forces surrounding us are many and they are fighting the battle of their lives.

CHAPTER TWO

The
STRANGE ACTS
of
GOD

> *"For bed is shorter than that man can stretch himself on it and the covering narrower than that can wrap himself in it. For the Lord shall rise up as in Mount Perazim, He shall be wroth as in the valley of Gideon, that He may do His work, His strange work and bring to pass His act, His strange act"* Isaiah 28: 20-21

Can you imagine a man of six feet tall, sleeping on a bench of about four feet; he would not be comfortable at all. Let us imagine a boy of seven years, who wants to sleep, use his mother's scarf as a covering; the scarf will not cover all the parts of his body. Some parts of his body will be exposed.

THE BOOK OF REVELATION

In these end times, there is a book that every believer ought to be reading. This is the last book of the Bible, Revelation. If you have not sat down to read the Book of Revelation, please, try and read it through. It is the timetable of God, concerning our age. It is an important book, can be called the grand finale of everything. Many people do not read it, because they regard it, as obscure and unclear. Whereas, the book is meant to reveal and unveil a lot of things to us. God will not write, what he does not want us to understand. If you do not study this book, you will miss out a lot of information.

Please, take a decision to read the book from now. Without this book, the scripture will not be complete. The Book of Revelation provides answers to a lot of questions about Christian life. It answers such questions as: Will sin continue? Will sorrow, death and pain go on? Where, exactly, are we in

God's plan? Is Christ coming to reign again, physically, in the world? What are we expecting before Christ comes again? What does 666, the mark of the Anti-Christ mean? Is the anti-Christ mark even in the world now? Will the world come to an end? Will the present heaven and earth exist forever? Are saints to spend eternity in heaven or on earth?

The answers to all these questions, can be found in the book. Many spectacular things had happened in this world, but nothing is going to be, as spectacular as, what you will find in Revelation, chapter 1verse7, when it begins to happen. Please, note that, no prophesy of the Bible has ever changed, and there is none that has failed. This passage says,

BEHOLD HE COMETH

"Behold, he cometh with clouds and every eye shall see him and they also which pierced him." All kindred of the earth shall wail because of him, Even so, Amen"

Nothing will match this verse, when it begins to happen. There are many believers, whom God has shown the vision of Christ coming back. We have come across such people, who have seen this revelation in dreams and in visions. They are enough evidence, and support of the truth of this revelation. This shows, that God is going around showing visions to people, that a time is coming, when all that will count is, what one has done with the Lord Jesus Christ, and not any other thing. It is, then, that people will understand the scriptures that "vanity upon vanity, all is vanity" Eccl.12: 8. People will then understand, that everything else that man is doing, is vanity. It is, then, it will begin to sound and appear strange, why some people run after the world.

These people run after the world, not knowing that they are running after vanity, leaving the reality. It is very strange, that many of the present day believers, pay much more attention to their bodies, than their spirits. These people feed their bodies with best foods, wear the best clothes, and take care of their bodies in so many ways, but neglect and starve the spirit, that will last forever. It is of no use to do so much to the body and neglect the spirit.

ENOCH'S RAPTURE

The flesh is not going to heaven, so, it is not interested in salvation. It, then, pulls people back from attending to their spirits. There are many signs in the Bible, the verse we read in Revelation, is about to come to pass. As a matter of fact, practically all the prophets in the Bible, talked about the second coming of Jesus Christ.

The first prophet in the Bible was Enoch. The Bible says, Enoch walked with God and he was not, because God took him and Enoch said, Jesus would come. Even at that early time of Genesi, other prophets like Jacob, Balaam, Zechariah, Jeremiah, Isaiah, Daniel, Joel, Amos, Micah etc all talked about the second coming of Jesus Christ. Jesus himself kept saying it many times in the New Testament. When Jesus went to heaven, physically, and the disciples were bothered and very worried, the Bible tells us that, some Angels stood by and said,

"Men of Galilee, why are you gazing at the sky? This same Jesus that has been taken away from you, will come back in like manner, as you have seen him going".

Those that pierced him, will cry on that day. Some believers can claim that they were not physically there, when Jesus was crucified and pierced, so they will easily absolve themselves from this prophecy. Piercing Jesus, by this scripture, is no longer a physical act, it is a spiritual thing.

FULFILLED SIGNS

The Bible says, after someone has known the way of salvation, tasted of the world to come, received the baptism of the Holy spirit, come to church and listened to messages, and after all these, falls away again, such a person is nailing Jesus on the cross the second time. These are the people, who are piercing Jesus on the cross.

All the signs that Jesus will soon come again, abound all around us. They include, signs like the false Christ, wars and rumors of war, famine and pestilences. Hatred is filling the earth, iniquity is abounding in the church, the love of many for God, is waxing cold and the gospel is being preached everywhere in the world, without exception. The signs of the days of Noah, which were merriment and pleasures, are now common thing. Violence has filled the whole world, people have become lovers of themselves; covetous, boastful, proud, blasphemous, and disobedient. They have the form of godliness, but deny the power of God.

NEGATIVE TRENDS

The Bible says, there will be increased satanic worship, and all sorts of negative things, to tell us that the end is very close.

Someone came to me in the church sometime ago, hid a charm in his pocket and was shaking it, hoping to harm me. This is an example of increased satanic activities. I felt sorry for him. If I had wanted to deal with him the Elijah way, I would have commanded all the charms in his pocket, to turn against him. People will hear the word of God many times, but they will still continue in their sins.

THE JUDGEMENT DAY

A time is coming when the bed will be too short and blanket too narrow, and secrets will be known. The present church is in a sorry state. Many times, we are called sons of God, instead of soldiers, because when one declares, that he is a soldier of Christ, it means he has laid down his life, and he is ready to die for Christ. Nobody joins the armed forces with a promise, or feeling, that he will not die.

The Bible says, "No man who warreth, entangleth himself with the affairs of this world; that he may please him who has appointed him as a soldier". Many People of the present generation, unfortunately, have never, really seen any revival. If we are not careful, we might not experience any revival before we go. This is, because of the way we are living our lives in this present day, by allowing the world to mould our lives for us.

One day, everybody will stand before Jehovah's throne. That day, the bed will be too short and the blanket will be too narrow, and the secrets of all hearts shall be revealed. Some people say " It is my life and I want to live it my own way" But, is it actually your own life? If God wants to withdraw it, you have no power to withhold it. People believe, they can do whatever they like with their hands, or legs, forgetting that, it was the hands and legs of Jesus that were pierced.

THE GREATEST MIRACLE

The greatest miracle one can receive, is the salvation of one's soul. If you fail to get saved here, or in any church, then, all other miracles are worthless and meaningless. I am aware that a lot of people come to Mountain of Fire and Miracle Ministries for miracles, but l implore them to get the first miracles, which is the miracle of salvation. Anything in your life, that will not make you get ready for heaven, or that will make you to be shaking before Jehovah's throne, will also prevent you from receiving your miracles from God. A lot of people have abandoned, what God has for them. They are looking after their personal things, running after business, contracts; etc while abandoning the main thing, that God has given them to do.

Somebody gave me a cassette some years ago, in which a brother who was said to be dead for six days, and later came alive, started to speak. He said many things about what he experienced, but there was one thing he said, which l will never forgot. He said he got to a particular place, and they brought out what they called the "Record of service." This record was surprisingly detailed. It had details like lateness to church, with two columns of faithfulness and disobedience, next was offering, Evangelism etc. Everything has been neatly planned out. He said, when it got to his turn, he looked at the book, and saw that in the area of tithes, he was marked faithful, but on offering, disobedience was marked for him.

ARE YOU SAVED

He wondered what happened, and he enquired. They took him through what he did, while he was alive. He was very worried. Anyway, he came back to life, because God instructed him to go and warn others. God has a controversy with the nations; and the Bible tells us that, God will start his judgment in the house of God. From the Book of Isaiah, it is clear that, it is alien for God to judge people, because it is said, " God will arise and do his strange work and carry out his strange act"

This shows, that, it is not something that God wants to do, but he has to do it. So, if you are reading this book, and you know that your life is not secured in the Lord Jesus or you are playing with sin, or you are playing with your salvation, you had better repented, and change now. Today, maybe the only day that God is giving you to do it right. After now, anything may happen to you, but the best thing is that, there is no point in continuing to live, when you are not sure, that your life is secured in the Lord Jesus Christ.

CHAPTER THREE

The **TRUTH YOU** CANNOT AVOID

"And I saw a great white throne, and him that sat on it, from whose face the earth and heaven fled away and there was found no place for them. And I saw the dead, small and great, stand before God and the books were opened, and another book was opened which is the book of life, and the dead were judged out of those things which were written in the books, according to their works. And the sea gave up the dead, which were in it, and death and hell delivered up the dead which were in them, and they were judge everyone according to their works. And death and hell were cast into the lake of fire. This is the second death. And whosoever was not found written in book of life was cast into the lake of fire" Revelation 20: 11-15

Whosoever here, refers to anybody and everybody, irrespective of position, or status; Pastor, Sunday school teacher, Evangelist, President, Director General, Engineer, Doctor, whosoever. As long as the person's name is not found in the book of life, such is cast into the lake of fire. This is the stand of God. God lifts up his curtain, for people to see the white throne. God and Jesus will be the judges, but one thing is certain, the judges of this world may make mistakes, but God will not make mistakes.

THE IMPENDING JUDGEMENT

There are many things we do not know now, and which are not clear to us, about what will happen at the end of the world, but one thing is certain, we know the judge, and he cannot make mistakes. A worldly lawyer, or judge could be bribed, to get a judgment of innocence, but this is not possible with God.

The purpose of the judgment, is to ensure that God gives due punishment to everyone, for the evil deeds, done. Now that you are still alive, God is giving you a trial before your condemnation. He is giving you ample opportunity, to decide and prove whether you want to go to heaven, or not. The Book of the Romans, Chapter 2 verses 1-16 show us, that the purposes of God's judgment is to judge the secrets of men (according to verse 16 of Romans, chapter 12) According to Matthew 12:36;

"But l say unto you, that every idle word that men speak, they shall give account thereof in the day of judgement."

The judgement is, to judge all the idle words that we speak. It is also to judge all the thoughts, words, actions and sins of men God has His own methods of administering judgement. For those, who did not hear the gospel before dying, God gave them a conscience, which is God's policeman, and there is no one without a conscience. Once, anyone does anything against his conscience, God will judge him, according to his conscience, even if such a person did not hear the gospel.

BE PREPARED

For those, who got the Law of Moses, followed the law and were able to fulfil the law, they will go to heaven, but those that failed by the law, will go to hell fire. Then, if you are exposed to the gospel like many of us are now, and we refused to hear and do accordingly, we shall also be judged, accordingly.

Behold, the Day of Judgment is approaching, when the bed will be too short and the blanket will be too narrow and it is necessary that we pray, that this day does not meet us unawares. Because of this, God has given us the Bible. This is now man's time to prove that he will go to heaven. The church is becoming worldly, and worldliness is going into the church, and all kinds of things are happening in the house of God.

THE JUDGEMENT THRONE

For example, a man of God was caught committing fornication with a church member. The same church now gave him a rousing send forth, after he was dismissed. This tells us that, those things that should not enter the church, have entered. A lot of preachers are confused, because many of the church members are wedded to sin. Whether you believe it or not, the judgment will come, anyway.

God will sit on His throne and the Bible says, the anger on his face will be so much, that heaven and earth will flee away from his sight and presence. All those, who have died from the time of Adam, all over the world, will show up, unbelievers will show up, too, backsliders, rebellious school children, those who say they have no time for the gospel now, children, who have reached the age of accountability, will be at the judgment seat of God. All those, who want to wait to achieve material success, before taking the worship of God seriously, will have themselves to blame, because they may never have the opportunity again. Now, is the time to prove to God, that you are worthy of heaven. There is no second chance at this judgment, and there is no room for repentance.

THE GREAT ROLL CALL

If a man remembers the name of Jesus on this day, the name will only torture him. Prayers will be too late and excuses, no matter how genuine and true, will not be acceptable. I would like to advise you now, if you are struggling with an unbeliever for something, drop the thing and let the unbeliever have it. This is because, there is no time, and if God calls anytime, and you are not able to give a proper answer, then, what will your going to church stands for?

There will be a great roll call, and those, who call themselves nominal Christians, attend beauty contests, watch TV as, if it were the Bible. Husbands, who run after their house helps at night, will all be present and their secrets shall be revealed. The judgment seat shall have no class, the high and low shall be merged together.

A day is coming, said the Lord, when the secret of all earth shall be revealed. One day, I was in a church and after the Sunday message, I noticed that somebody was making a noise outside, threatening to beat up another person and people were begging her to be calm, and not to beat the person. It took me time to realise that I was the one she wanted to beat up. Why? She told the people that somebody must have told me about her secrets, which I used to preach. I, too, started to beg her not to beat me up. This same person, unfortunately, is dead now. Those things, of which the Lord was speaking to her to repent from, eventually, killed her.

HYPOCRITES IN THE CHURCH

When you die, you appear in another world. The Bible says, "It is given unto men to die once, after that, is judgment". Every hidden atrocity, cleverly concealed sins, and hidden lusts will be exposed on this day. All the people who are spiritual submarines will be known. Some people come to church and behave as, if they are serving the pastor. Some try to, physically, avoid the men of God, because they know that their activities are unclean, they keep other immoral books at home, only to carry the Bible to church for camouflage.

If you are in this category of people, you are doing yourself a great harm. All these will be revealed that day. The parable of the dog, going back to its vomit will, then, be applicable to you. You should not be interested in the honour of man, or earthly posts. You should be interested in the honour of God and seek after it diligently.

A lot of people, who come to church, are not interested in personal spiritual growth, and in spite of the messages, they still do not change their ways of life. They feel sober, when in church, but go back to those things they felt bad about, as soon after they leave the church. Whereas the Bible says, "Shall we continue in sin that grace may about? God forbid."

TWO DEATHS

Miracles cannot multiply, when we remain in sin. The devil keeps running after people, because they possess his property. You have to repent. If you were to stand now, before the judgment seat of Christ, what would you say? There are only two ways, the broad way and the narrow way. There is no centre. The broad way leads to hell, and the narrow way leads to glory. There are only two types of people; the saved sinners and the unsaved sinners. The Bible calls them, the sheep and the goat, or the living and the dead.

There are only two deaths, the death of the righteous and the death of the wicked. There are only two futures, the kingdom of heaven and hell fire. These days, a lot of people want to copy the fashion of the world, which the Bible describes as "fading away".

The devil has taken hold of the literature of the world, and he is using all the funny pornographic magazines to confuse people. Parents should be careful of the type of materials that circulate in their homes, so that God will not judge them, for confusing their children.

Anything not good for the youths, is not better for the adults. It is a shame to our society, that the best selling magazines and materials are the sexiest ones. Many churches are beautiful outwardly, but within, they contain the bones of dead men. God is tired of lip services. He wants heart services. God will not expect benchwarmers, but only true worshippers. Do not be like the proverbial frog, that wanted to fly on borrowed wings. He hit the rock and fell down. Do not live your life on borrowed spiritual wings. Your faith cannot rely on some one else's own. You have to develop yourself personally; your relationship with God must be personal.

DESTRUCTIVE TRINITIES

There is what we call trinity of spiritual failure - Money, Alcohol and Sex. If any of these are in your life, then, be assured, that you are on a direct expressway to hell fire. There is trinity of defeat, comprising Doubt, Worry and Fear. If you entertain any of these, you are going to hell.

The master of the trinities is the trinity of destruction, which comprises-Sin, Death and Hell. If you love yourself, you must hate these triplets. There is no accident on the way, that is so broad and wide. The good news is, God has not made provision for anyone to perish, so the decision to perish is personal. On the Day of Judgment, the bed will be too short and the blanket too narrow. Every concealed secrets, shall be exposed to all.

Every evil deed will be exposed. Some people have the call of God upon their lives, but they are joking and playing with it. Some of us are seeking recognition that God does not want them to seek. A lot of people carry fake smiles on their faces, even when, they are not happy. For all these people, on that day, the bed will be too short and the blanket will be too narrow. If you have any sin to confess, confess it to the Holy Spirit now, repent and beg for forgiveness. You can also deceive yourself if you want to, by pretending that you have no sin. Please, readjust yourself and rededicate your life to God

PRAYER POINTS
1. I rebuke the spirit of backsliding, in Jesus name.
2. Father Lord, anything that will remove me from your presence, take it away from me, in the name of Jesus.
3. Fire of God, purge away every filthiness from my spirit, in the name of Jesus.
4. Oh Lord, give me power to subdue the flesh, in the name of Jesus.
5. Oh Lord, give me the grace to focus on the Lord Jesus, all the time.

6. Father Lord, help me to be heavenly minded all the days of my life, in the name of Jesus
7. Oh Lord, give me the grace to love you and cling unto you, in the Lord Jesus.
8. I withdraw myself from the camp of the enemies of God, in the name of Jesus.
9. Let the word of God prosper in my life, in the name of Jesus.
10. Father Lord, remove from me every problem that sin has brought into my life, in the name of Jesus.
11. I reject the spirit of rebellion, in the name of Jesus.

CHAPTER FOUR

THE WOLVES, *Serpents,* SCORPIONS

> *"Behold, I send you forth as sheep in the midst of wolves: be ye therefore wise as serpents, and harmless as doves."* Matthew 10: 16

In this passage, Jesus is warning us about the danger surrounding us in the world. The wolf is a very dangerous animal. Physically, if a contest were declared between the sheep and the wolf, the sheep would stand no chance at all, because the wolf is stronger. The wolf would destroy the sheep utterly.

The environment in which we find ourselves is very hostile. The Bible does not use kind words to describe it. The Bible talks about the environment being filled with serpents, scorpions, lions, foxes and all kinds of terrible creatures. And, in the passage we read, the Bible is talking about wolves. Truly, the wolf can destroy the sheep, but there is something that can enter the sheep, give it the ability to confront, and defeat the wolf. That thing, is the Spirit of the living God. The Holy Spirit can enter the sheep because of certain qualities, found in the sheep.

THE POWER OF THE SPIRIT

Readers of the Bible, recognise that Samson was a man, who did exploits. There was a time he met a lion on the way. The lion did not know that Samson was not just an ordinary human being, it could devour. It smiled at Samson and wanted to pounce on him but then, something was in the life of Samson, which the lion did not know about. The Spirit of the Lord was mightily upon Samson.

> *"Then went Samson down, and his father and his mother to Timnath: and came to the*

> *vineyards of Timnath: and behold, a young lion roared against him. And the Spirit of the Lord came mightily upon him, and he rent him as he would rent a kid, and he had nothing in his hand: but he told not his father or his mother what he had done."* Judges 14: 5-6

The Spirit of the Lord came upon Samson.

When the Spirit of the Lord comes upon men, new things begin to happen. When it comes upon you, new ideas would begin to come up in your mind, a new power would enter into your spirit, you would begin to resist the devil, and he would, certainly, flee from you. Perhaps, as you are reading this book, you are the timid and fearful type, when that Spirit comes upon you, it will make you to become bold. Samson did not flee from the lion, instead he pounced on it. Meaning that, he did to the lion, what the lion planned to do to him.

The Spirit of God has always been doing wonders in people's lives, and I am sure, He would do wonders in yours, too, in the name of Jesus. Every serious man of God in the Bible, passed through this kind of experience that we are talking about. The seventy elders had a difficult task to do. Ordinarily, they would not have been able to cope, but God had to do something to them, before pushing them into the midst of wolves.

We, too, need this Spirit to give us wisdom. We need Him, to disgrace all the lions, harassing us. Gideon, too, was a man that was called by God, for a task he could not ordinarily cope with, until the same Spirit came upon him. The same thing happened to king David, Simon in the New Testament, and to all the apostles. The Spirit of the living God, came upon them and that made all the difference.

THREE SEGMENTS

The whole of the Bible can be divided into three clear sections:

Section 1: The Time of Tabernacles and Temples:

The people of Israel, built tabernacles in the wilderness. Anytime they were moving, they carried their tabernacle. When they finished with tabernacles, they started building temples. That time, God was in a place and not in their lives. This is the reason, the devil was able to mess people up thoroughly, in the Old Testament. God was inside the tabernacles and inside the temples, but was not inside their lives. The high priest used to go to the Holy of holies, once a year He did that with very great precautions, because anything could happen to him there. That was what we experienced in the Old Testament.

Section 2: The time of Jesus Christ:

Jesus came, men looked upon Him and decided that, He was not worthy to remain alive, so, they got rid of Him. But, before then, He moved around preaching the gospel and healing the sick. God anointed Him with power and He did great exploits. He laid the foundation of the apostolic ministry. When He was going away, He said, "I am going away but I will not leave you comfortless. I will send you another Comforter," and that ushered us into the realm of the Holy Spirit, where we are now.

Section 3: The ministry of the Holy Spirit:

The ministry of the Holy Spirit, is the last ministry. It is the Spirit, that allows us to live in the supernatural. What I am talking about, surpasses just speaking in tongues. There are many people, who speak in tongues, which has no power. What I am talking about, is moving in the supernatural. Sometime ago, a certain woman attended a service, where somebody prayed on anointing oil, which she drank. Shortly after, she pressed to go to the toilet, where she excreted three snakes, not worms. That is what you call, moving in the supernatural. There are some sisters in our fellowship, who have never been to any school in their lives, but they can read the Bible very well. That is what you call, moving in the supernatural. This is the only thing, that can confront, and defeat the wolf.

Our country used to be in terrible darkness and many evil things were happening. Clergymen used to go to evil people to collect power. People were even afraid to call the names of witches. All kinds of horrible things were happening, until some men, who had the Spirit of the living God, came and confronted the wolves. You cannot confront the wolves, when you are chewing gum in the church, or when you cannot concentrate during service.

CHAPTER FIVE

The BAPTISM of the HOLY SPIRIT

Baptism of the Holy Spirit, in the right sense of it, is an experience that revolutionises people's lives. Many years ago, I was passing by a university campus, around 1.00 a.m. when I saw three girls wearing tight trousers, standing. As I was wondering what they were doing there, they waved me down, I stopped and I asked, what they were doing there. They said, they were looking for transport to take them home, I offered to help them.

As I was driving, I asked them again, what they were doing there at that hour and they said, they were coming from a party that had just ended. I went on further to tell them that, it was dangerous for them to be there at that time and they replied, "Sir, Jesus will protect us." When I heard that, I asked, "Are you born again?" They said, "Yes." So, I asked again, "If you are born again, then, what are you doing in a night party, and dressed the way you are?" They said, "We are not only born again, but also filled with the Holy Spirit."

SELF DECEPTION

I said, "Supposing Jesus comes and meets you in that party, dancing with unbelievers, what do you think would happen?" One of them said, "No. He cannot come now, because I am not yet married, and I have not done anything. He would have to wait for me to finish everything, then, He can come." It is really a pity. A lot of people, who claim to have the baptism of the Holy Spirit, are not serious, yet. If you received the genuine baptism of the Holy Spirit, it would revolutionise your life. It would turn your life upside down for good. It would reverse your situation.

For us to disgrace the present-day wolves, we need the power of the Holy Spirit. One man of God said, the sign of Christianity is not a cross, but a tongue of fire. When the fire comes upon your life, things begin to happen. The greatest reason we need fresh fire from above, is for us to be a great burnt offering for God. Once you become that kind of burnt offering, the first thing that would disappear from your life is the fear of death. Immediately, the devil sees, that you are no longer afraid of death, he would flee from you, because there is no other greater thing, with which he can threaten you.

A BURNT OFFERING

Supposing the Holy Spirit wakes you up at 2. 00 a.m. and says, "Son, or daughter, today I have a message for you to deliver at the front gate of Atan Cemetery." What would you do? Somebody, who is on fire for God, will not think of the danger, but would go there. That is what we mean by being a great burnt offering for the Lord. People, who have got to that level, are above fear. When such people are threatened with charms, they ask the person issuing the threat, to bring his/her most powerful one.

When we become a great burnt offering for God, it is then, we can disgrace the wolves and when God is looking for someone to rely upon, He can depend on us. The question now is; "Do you have that fire of God, burning in you?" The Bible says, that our God is a consuming fire, and when that fire comes on you, you will have liberty in the spirit.

When some people speak in tongues, it would appear as, if somebody was squeezing their throat, and quenching the power. I pray that we may have the fire that John spoke about. Then, the devil, sin, sicknesses cannot live in our lives, because it would be too hot. This is why, we need the fresh fire of the Holy Spirit. Many have quenched that fire by their words, unbelief, and the unwillingness to change. It is time to check your baptism again. Does it have fire in it? Or have you lost it?

PERFECT LOVE

The second reason why we need fresh fire is, that we may be perfected in love. You must love all sinners, not wishing that any should perish. Paul said, "Though I preach the gospel, I have nothing to glory of, but necessity is laid upon me. Woe is me, if I preach not the gospel." He was able to say that, because something had happened to him.

The third reason we need fresh fire is, for holy zeal to fall upon us. The apostles had fire, and they got result. A friend of mine in England, was invited to Russia to preach. He did not understand their language. He preached in English, while another person interpreted in Russian language. His message was on, why we have redundant people in the house of God. He said, that those, who are redundant in the house of God, should be rendered more redundant.

The message touched his interpreter so much that, the man broke down and could not interpret any more. Then, suddenly, the Spirit of the living God fell upon my friend, and for half an hour, he preached in Russian language and there was not a single sinner at that meeting, who did not give his life to Jesus.

Immediately, the half an hour was over, he did not know, what he was saying again. He just saw that sinners coming out to give their lives to Christ. That is what the Holy Spirit could do in one's life.

Beloved, we need to pray that the fire of the Holy Spirit, should fall upon us, by praying the following prayer points, aggressively.

PRAYER POINTS

1. Anything hindering the move of the Holy Spirit in my life, release me now, in the name of Jesus.

2. Holy Ghost fire, move freely in my life, in the name of Jesus.

3. Let the Holy Ghost fire, purge my life, in the name of Jesus.

4. Anything quenching the fire of God in my life, die by fire, in the name of Jesus.

5. Let the fire of the Lord, consume every darkness in my life, in Jesus' name.

6. O Lord, make my life invisible to demonic observers, in the name of Jesus.

7. I cancel every evil vow, affecting my life, negatively, in the name of Jesus.

CHAPTER SIX

An *UNFORGETTABLE* ENCOUNTER

> *"And there were certain Greeks among them, that came up to worship at the feast. The same came therefore to Philip, which was of Bethsaida of Galilee, and desired him, saying, Sir, we would see Jesus. Philip cometh and telleth Andrew: and again Andrew and Philip tell Jesus. And Jesus answered them saying, the hour is come, that the Son of man should be glorified. Verily, verily, I say unto you, Except a corn of wheat fall into the ground and die, it abideth alone: but if it die, it bringeth forth much fruit. He that loveth his life shall lose it; and he that hateth his life in this world shall keep it unto life eternal. If any man serve me, let him follow me; and where I am, there shall also my servant be: if any man serve me, him will my Father honour."* John 12: 20 - 26

Certain Greeks came, to an annual religious feast in Jerusalem. They saw men there practicing religion. They looked at everything, followed all the rituals, attended all the meetings, but were careful enough to note that in all these ceremonies, something was missing. They were still empty. But there was somebody in town, who had the real thing, so, they began to ask: "Sir, we will see Jesus." You may ask what their motive was. Maybe it was curiosity, or that they wanted to get something out of Jesus, or they wanted to solve a problem, or they just desired to know this man, that people were talking about, or they decided to encounter the truth in reality.

Having an encounter with the Lord, or the experience of seeing Jesus, is fundamental to genuine Christian experience. The reason some people backslide, or are not able to appreciate their salvation, is due to lack of this encounter. Sometimes, people backslide, because they have never seen the Man of Galilee. The day God opens your spiritual eyes, see Him hanging on the cross, with blood dripping down, and suffering, the reality will dawn on you, and all other things will be insignificant. The experience of seeing Jesus, is fundamental to the Christian faith.

TWO TYPES OF PEOPLE IN THE CAMP OF GOD
In the camp of the Lord, you can see two types of people.

1. Those who have met the Lord.

2. Those who have met the church. That is, those who practice church, or religion.

Those who have not met the Lord, lose their temper easily. For example, when they go somewhere and somebody takes up their seat, they would shout, "Get up from there, do you know when I arrived here. Get away." They know how to pray fire prayer, but have not met the Lord. This is a tragedy.

A time will come, when all those proclaiming to be Christians, shall be distributed into two clear camps. The first group, is the group of the goats, and the second group, is the group of the sheep. The Bible says, that eventually, the goats would be cast away into the lake of fire. This is, because they did not really encounter the Lord. But if you want to encounter the Lord in reality, there is an essential condition, that regulates such an encounter. We can find that in the response of Jesus to the request, "Sir, we would see Jesus," in John 12: 24. It says, "Verily, verily, I say unto you, except a corn of wheat fall into the ground, and die, it abideth alone: but if it die, it bringeth forth much fruit." Herein lies the spiritual law, that regulates God's dealings with men, for God is a God of law. This has nothing to do with your post, or qualification. It has nothing to do with being a pastor, having attended Bible colleges, or having studied theology.

CARNAL KNOWLEDGE

Several years ago, a man, who had a Ph.D in Bible Knowledge, was invited to a Christian meeting somewhere in Ebute-Metta, Lagos. The meeting was filled with illiterates, carpenters and bricklayers and market men and women. He was supposed to give them a lecture on knowing God. He started by telling them the meaning of the phrase 'to know.' He spent about fifteen minutes on that, and then went further to explain "God" for another fifteen minutes. After this, he went into the lecture proper and gave a beautiful lecture.

But, when he finished, one carpenter who did not even attend any school said, "Excuse me, sir, I have a question for you. Have you met Jesus yourself? Can you claim, that you have experienced Him?" The Ph.D teacher, did not understand what the man was asking him, so, he replied, "I am sorry, I don't have an answer to that question." The carpenter now sat him down, and gave him a lecture on practical Christianity. The lecturer was trying to teach others about the man he did not know. God is a God of law, and He works by divine principles. When you discover these principles and comply with them, it will bring you into line with God's will.

God Himself has a pattern. Everything in heaven is well patterned. If God gives you a little opportunity, of seeing heavenly organisation, you will not want to stay on earth anymore. There is nothing on earth, that is as beautiful and orderly as in heaven. This was why God told Moses, "And look that thou make them
after their pattern, which was shewed thee in the mount" (Exodus 25: 40). This means that, if Moses had decided not to follow the pattern, nothing would have happened.

People write to me suggesting that the MFM should use drums, and allow people to dress the way they like, even if it means dressing indecently, so that more people can come. I always tell them, that it was not the pattern shown to me, and that I prefer to stick to the divine pattern given by God.

THE PERIL OF DISOBEDIENCE

Listening to such proposals, would be tantamount to disobedience. If you want to build a house, and you look around, see one that you really like, and want to fashion yours after it, that would become your model. So, the only way that we are ever going to see Jesus here, and in the world to come, is by dying to self. John 24: 12 says, "Except a corn of wheat falls into the ground and die, it abideth alone. But if it die, it bringeth forth much fruit."

In Exodus 33, we read about an interesting encounter. Moses knew, that the Israelites were a very stubborn, and proud people. He was meant to take them to the Promised land. He knew what he had faced with Pharaoh, and knew that he could not go by his own strength. He realised the impossibility of the task, unless God Himself went with him.

Verses 13 - 15: "Now therefore, I pray thee, if I have found grace in thy sight, shew me now thy way, that I may know thee, that I may find grace in thy sight: and consider that this nation is thy people. And he said, My presence shall go with thee, and I will give thee rest. And he (Moses) said unto him, If thy presence go not with me, carry us not up hence." Verses 18 - 19: "And he said, I beseech thee, shew me thy glory. And he said, I will make all my goodness pass before thee, and I will proclaim the name of the Lord before thee; and will be gracious to whom I will be gracious, and will shew mercy on whom I will shew mercy." There is an ancient powerful hymn by one man called, Wesley, which says,

"To thee O Lord of love, I bow and I prostrate at your feet. By faith, I am seeing you passing now, but now, I ask for more. A glimpse of you may not suffice but I want your presence. I cannot see your face and live. Then, let me see your face, and die."

WE MUST SEE JESUS

This song means, that his longing to see Jesus, was more important than life itself. Herein, then lies the great truth. No man can see the face of the Lord, unless he is prepared to fall into the ground like a corn of wheat, and die.

Prophet Isaiah saw God, and his life was never the same. But, before, then, he had unclean lips (Isaiah 6). When he saw the

Lord, he became what is known as the messianic prophet. Some people also call him the evangelist of the Old Testament, because in the Book of Isaiah, you see the gospel clearly preached, and also the prophecies about the Lord Jesus Christ. Twice in Isaiah, chapter six, he said, "I saw the Lord." Having seen the Lord, then, he saw himself. And when he saw the Lord, he said, "I am undone, I am a man of unclean lips. I live in the midst of people with unclean lips." He knew, who he was. And, immediately he identified his problem, the Lord said, "Yes, now you are ready. You seraphim, take a coal of fire and drop it on his dirty tongue, and purge his sins out." This was foretelling the moment when the Holy Spirit, would take coals from the altar of Calvary, and take away our sins. When this happened to Isaiah, another request went forth: "Who shall I send, who will go for us. Then, he said, Here I am, send me." The only man, qualified to go, was the man, who had died; the man who had seen Jesus. This is very important.

HAVE YOU SEEN THE LORD

The reason, some people are busy criticizing others, instead of looking at themselves, is probably because they have not seen the Lord. The big truth is, that you, really, cannot see yourself, clearly, until you have seen the Lord. Have you encountered the Almighty God?

Have you really encountered the "I AM?" If you have encountered Him, your life wiill be reversed. Some of the things, that are so important to others, will lose their significance in your sight. All you would be interested in is, just serving the Lord at all cost. Even, if you have to be sweeping the floor, it does not matter, you still have to please the master. Saul of Tarsus was a sincere man, but he was sincerely wrong. He was educated, theologically and doctrinally sound, but he had one serious sickness- he had never met the Lord. "Sir, we would see Jesus."

Experiencing, or encountering the Lord, is different from going to church. A person could sit in the church, until he wears his bottom out on the seat, and not meet the Lord. He could meet people, have church post, be extravagant and flamboyant, but never, really, met the Lord. He cannot point to an experience, where he had encountered the Master.

Once you have seen the Lord, no problem will stand before you. No problem can stay, where Jesus is. When you have seen the Lord, who is a witch, that can stand before you? When you have seen the Lord, spirit husband, spirit wife, or familiar spirit, cannot withstand you. What is sickness, when the Lord is standing? Something happened to Paul, on his way to Damascus. He saw Jesus, and died. So, he, who was pursuing Christians, now began to preach the same gospel, that he hated so much and wanted to terminate. Therefore, the road to Damascus, became the personal Calvary of Paul.

YOUR CALVARY

What is your own personal Calvary? When did you die? Is Jesus living in you now? Has your anger died? Has your bitterness died? Has your unforgiving spirit died? Where, and when is your own Calvary? When did the old pass away in your life? When did your Saul die, to give birth to Paul? When Paul became a new man, preached the gospel? Paul saw Jesus, and died. No wonder, a songwriter says, "It is no longer I that liveth but Christ that liveth in me." John the apostle, the writer of the book of Revelation, saw Jesus and his life was never the same. You can observe that right from the first chapter of the book.

Sometime ago, we had a powerful meeting, lasting three days with dry fasting. The meeting was for people, who desired spiritual gifts. Such meetings were usually started with a prayer point like:

"O Lord, give me the spirit of prophecy." On that very day, we prayed so hard, that most participants, began to prophesy.

AN ANGELIC VISITOR

The Lord opened the eyes of one sister, for the first time. I found that, occasionally, the sister would look at the back, and quickly turn her face again to the front. Apparently, she was seeing something. When we closed the service, she came to me and said, "Excuse me, sir, immediately, we started praying, one giant man in a white garment was standing at our back with his face shining like fire."

I knew she had seen the angel of the living God. As this same sister was going home, she decided to visit one of her friends, who happened to be her prayer partner. When she got there, her friend served her some food, which she rejected since she wanted to break her fast at home. She looked into the eyes of her friend, and discovered that there was no black pupil inside them. Everything was white. She was very surprised, because that was somebody she had been praying with for six years. When God opened her eyes, she, then, discovered that she had been praying with her enemies.

There is no point going about with blind eyes now. There is no need for you to employ a secretary, who will be putting blood inside your tea, and you are drinking it, and thanking God for the tea girl. Stephen, in Acts 7: 54- 60 said,

"When they heard these things, they were cut to the heart, and they gnashed on him with their teeth. But, he, being full of the Holy Ghost, looked up, steadfastly, into heaven and saw the glory of God and Jesus, standing on the right hand of God. Then, they cried out with a loud voice, stopped their ears, and ran upon him with one accord, casting him out of the city, and stoned him. The witnesses laid down their clothes at a young man's feet, whose name was Saul. As, they stoned Stephen, he called upon God, saying, Lord Jesus, receive my spirit. He kneeled down, cried with a loud voice, Lord, lay not this sin to their charge, and when he had said this, he fell asleep." They stoned him to death, but their purposes were defeated, just like in Calvary; instead of destroying the testimony of Jesus, those who, crucified Him magnified it.

Anyone persecuting a Christian, is only asking for an explosion. In his death, Stephen cried out like Jesus, "Father, forgive them, for they know not what they are doing." By this, Stephen became a corn of wheat, that fell into the ground, and died. You, really, have to pray harder now, because men are doing very strange things.

A sister told me, that a fetish priest asked her to do a ritual. He asked her to put a standard coffin inside a Mercedes Benz V-boot car, and drive it right into the sea. I asked her what that action would bring out, and she said, it would bring breakthroughs. I asked her, if she had done it, she said, "yes". Wicked men are waxing stronger and stronger, and they are becoming very clever in their operations. There is evil wisdom in operation, all over the place. It is time for deliverance ministers to be able to look straight into a satanic agent's eyes and say, "Oga, that thing you tried last time, do not try it again. If you do, you will die." The satanic agent will know, that an authority is talking, and will apologise.

Why is it that many people, who desire to encounter Jesus, do not succeed him?
Why is it, that some people cry out loud, and it seems as, if Jesus is far. Let us consider some of the reasons for this:

1. **Stain in the mind:** Our mind is like a stage, where there are actors, acting.

Some thoughts are good, and some are bad. Sometimes, we cannot prevent certain thoughts from making an entrance to the stage of our minds, but we have the power to either make them play on, or throw them off the stage. Therefore, the first step in committing sin that will block, the eyes of someone from seeing Jesus, is to indulge in the thoughts, that are not pleasing to God. The evil thoughts that do not please the Lord, start from the heart.

The act of sinning itself, starts from the mind. Once you are committing sin in your thought, it is as simple as committing it, physically. The Bible says, that if you lust after a woman in your heart, there is no difference between you and a person, who commits it, physically. The state of our minds may be hidden to others, but it is not hidden to God. We indulge in many evil thoughts, that we ourselves would not even allow people to know about. It is also on this stage of our mind, that battles, that will determine our destiny are fought. The powers of darkness like this stage of our minds.

2. **Wearing mask:** Masks conceal the true identity of people. It is the spirit of pretence, false claim and false profession.

A person, who wears a mask, becomes a stranger even to himself. It is possible to see somebody in the church, holding a pen and a book in his hands, and, yet, he is sleeping, and you will not know. He is wearing a mask. Such a person will say amen in the wrong places. A certain man was sleeping, as a preacher was preaching. Suddenly, the preacher said, anyone that wanted to go to hell fire, should stand up. This man, who was sleeping, woke up and stood up. He found, that he was the only one standing up. Everybody was surprised. He was sleeping, when the major part of the sentence was made. He only heard stand up, and he stood up. Mask wearers claim to be super spiritual, when they are nothing.

The Lord, likes people, such as the blind man in John, Chapter Nine whom He healed. Because he was blind, he did not even know the man, who healed him. When Jesus met him in the temple, and asked him, saying, "Believeth you the Son of man?" He said, "Who is he Lord, that I may believe him?" He did not know, and was quite ready to admit. When he was told, that the man who opened his eyes was a sinner, he said, "I know that God heareth not sinners." They shouted at him, to shut up, and asked if, he now wanted to teach them the Bible. "This man is wrong; why should He heal you on the Sabbath day?" they said. The man who was healed said, "It is wonderful that a sinner could open blind eyes," and they threw him out.

3. Bitterness and resentment: If you have any of these, it will blind your spiritual eyes, and you will not see anything.

4. Living in the past: Some people spend the whole of their time living in the past. Such people would say, "If not for that foolish man, who made me pregnant in form three, I would not have been here." "If not for the wicked parents, who did not send me to school, I would have been a graduate now." How can you allow the mistake, that you made twenty-eight years ago, to be controlling your life now, when you know, that Jesus has forgiven you?

5. Carnality: Romans 8: 6 says, "For to be carnally minded is death: but to be spiritually minded is life and peace." If, as you read this message, you are still going to unbelievers' parties, dancing their dance and celebrating their ceremonies, you are a carnal Christian.

6. Negative attitudes: A lot of people have negative attitudes towards everything. The world is filled with self-appointed judges, and self-appointed referees, who criticise others, endlessly.

7. Men pleasers: There are people, who think, that they must have the praise and approval of others, regardless of the cost. Yet, Jesus said, "Woe unto you, when men say that you are good." You are invited to where you should not go, but because you are afraid of offending somebody, you say, "Yes, I will go." Men pleasers! Such people, spend a lot of time thinking of what people think about them, or what people expect from them. The thought of what people would say, has produced a lot of spiritual tragedies. For you to please men always, you must wear a mask. I would like to let you know, that if, you have not pursued your Christianity to a level, where someone has called you a fanatic, you have not started. They told Jesus, that He was demon possessed. They also told Paul, that he was mad. Therefore, beloved, it is time to seek an encounter with the Lord. Job 42: 5 -6: "I have heard of thee, by the hearing of the ear: but, now mine eye seeth thee. Wherefore, I abhor myself, and repent in dust and ashes."

Prayer points

1. O Lord, I want to experience you, in the name of Jesus.

2. O Lord, I want to see you, know you, and experience you, in the name of Jesus.

3. Anything hindering me from seeing the Lord, fall down, and die, in Jesus' name.

4. I refuse to live in darkness, in the name of Jesus.

5. I reject spiritual blindness and spiritual deafness, in the name of Jesus.

6. Let every spiritual cataract clear away from my

eyes, in the name of Jesus.

7. Father Lord, I want to see you, in the name of Jesus.

OTHER BOOKS BY DR. D. K. OLUKOYA
- 20 Marching Orders To Fulfill Your Destiny
- 30 Things The Anointing Can Do For You
- 30 Prophetic Arrows From Heaven
- A-Z of Complete Deliverance
- Abraham's Children in Bondage
- Basic Prayer Patterns
- Be Prepared
- Bewitchment must die
- Biblical Principles of Dream Interpretation
- Born Great, But Tied Down
- Breaking Bad Habits
- Breakthrough Prayers For Business Professionals
- Bringing Down The Power of God
- Brokenness
- Can God Trust You?
- Can God?
- Command The Morning
- Connecting to The God of Breakthroughs
- Consecration Commitment & Loyalty
- Contending For The Kingdom
- Criminals In The House Of God
- Dancers At The Gate of Death
- Dealing With The Evil Powers Of Your Father's House
- Dealing With Tropical Demons

- Dealing With Local Satanic Technology
- Dealing With Witchcraft Barbers
- Dealing With Unprofitable Roots
- Dealing With Hidden Curses
- Dealing With Destiny Vultures
- Dealing With Satanic Exchange
- Dealing With Destiny Thieves
- Deliverance Of The Head
- Deliverance: God's Medicine Bottle
- Deliverance From Spirit Husband And Spirit Wife
- Deliverance From The Limiting Powers
- Deliverance From Evil Foundation
- Deliverance of The Brain
- Deliverance Of The Conscience
- Deliverance By Fire
- Destiny Clinic
- Destroying Satanic Masks
- Disgracing Soul Hunters
- Divine Yellow Card
- Divine Prescription For Your Total Immunity
- Divine Military Training
- Dominion Prosperity
- Drawers Of Power From The Heavenlies
- Evil Appetite
- Evil Umbrella

- Facing Both Ways
- Failure In The School Of Prayer
- Fire For Life's Journey
- For We Wrestle ...
- Freedom Indeed
- Healing Through Prayers
- Holiness Unto The Lord
- Holy Fever
- Holy Cry
- Hour Of Decision
- How To Obtain Personal Deliverance
- How To Pray When Surrounded By The Enemies
- I Am Moving Forward
- Idols Of The Heart
- Igniting Your Inner Fire
- Igniting Your Inner Fire
- Is This What They Died For?
- Kill Your Goliath By Fire
- Killing The Serpent of Frustration
- Let God Answer By Fire
- Let Fire Fall
- Limiting God
- Lord, Behold Their Threatening
- Madness Of The Heart
- Making Your Way Through The Traffic Jam of Life

- Meat For Champions
- Medicine For Winners
- My Burden For The Church
- Open Heavens Through Holy Disturbance
- Overpowering Witchcraft
- Paralysing The Riders And The Horse
- Personal Spiritual Check-Up
- Possessing The Tongue of Fire
- Power To Recover Your Birthright
- Power Against Coffin Spirits
- Power Against Unclean Spirits
- Power Against The Mystery of Wickedness
- Power Against Destiny Quenchers
- Power Against Dream Criminals
- Power Against Local Wickedness
- Power Against Marine Spirits
- Power Against Spiritual Terrorists
- Power To Recover Your Lost Glory
- Power To Disgrace The Oppressors
- Power Must Change Hands
- Power To Shut Satanic Doors
- Power Against The Mystery of Wickedness
- Power of Brokenness
- Pray Your Way To Breakthroughs
- Prayer To Make You Fulfill Your Divine Destiny

- Prayer Strategies For Spinsters And Bachelors
- Prayer Warfare Against 70 Mad Spirits
- Prayer Is The Battle
- Prayer To Kill Enchantment
- Prayer Rain
- Prayers To Destroy Diseases And Infirmities
- Prayers For Open Heavens
- Prayers To Move From Minimum To Maximum
- Praying Against Foundational Poverty
- Praying Against The Spirit Of The Valley
- Praying In The Storm
- Praying To Dismantle Witchcraft
- Praying To Destroy Satanic Roadblocks
- Principles Of Prayer
- Raiding The House of The Strongman
- Release From Destructive Covenants
- Revoking Evil Decrees
- Safeguarding Your Home
- Satanic Diversion of the Black Race
- Secrets of Spiritual Growth & Maturity
- Seventy Rules of Spiritual Warfare
- Seventy Sermons To Preach To Your Destiny
- Silencing The Birds Of Darkness
- Slave Masters
- Slaves Who Love Their Chains

- Smite The Enemy And He Will Flee
- Speaking Destruction Unto The Dark Rivers
- Spiritual Education
- Spiritual Growth And Maturity
- Spiritual Warfare And The Home
- Stop Them Before They Stop You
- Strategic Praying
- Strategy Of Warfare Praying
- Students In The School Of Fear
- Symptoms Of Witchcraft Attack
- Taking The Battle To The Enemy's Gate
- The Amazing Power of Faith
- The Vagabond Spirit
- The Unlimited God
- The Wealth Transfer Agenda
- The Way Of Divine Encounter
- The Unconquerable Power
- The Baptism of Fire
- The Battle Against The Spirit Of Impossibility
- The Chain Breaker
- The Dinning Table Of Darkness
- The Enemy Has Done This
- The Evil Cry Of Your Family Idol
- The Fire Of Revival
- The School of Tribulation

- The Gateway To Spiritual Power
- The Great Deliverance
- The Internal Stumbling Block
- The Lord Is A Man Of War
- The Mystery Of Mobile Curses
- The Mystery Of The Mobile Temple
- The Prayer Eagle
- The University of Champions
- The Power of Aggressive Prayer Warriors
- The Power of Priority
- The Tongue Trap
- The Terrible Agenda
- The Scale of The Almighty
- The Hidden Viper
- The Star In Your Sky
- The star hunters
- The Spirit Of The Crab
- The Snake In The Power House
- The Slow Learners
- The University of Champions
- The Skeleton In Your Grandfather's Cupboard
- The Serpentine Enemies
- The Secrets Of Greatness
- The Seasons Of Life
- The Pursuit Of Success

- Tied Down In The Spirits
- Too Hot To Handle
- Turnaround Breakthrough
- Unprofitable Foundations
- Victory Over Your Greatest Enemies
- Victory Over Satanic Dreams
- Violent Prayers Against Stubborn Situations
- War At The Edge Of Breakthroughs
- Wasted At The Market Square of Life
- Wasting The Wasters
- Wealth Must Change Hands
- What You Must Know About The House Fellowship
- When the Battle is from Home
- When You Need A Change
- When The Deliverer Need Deliverance
- When Things Get Hard
- When You Are Knocked Down
- When You Are Under Attack
- When The Enemy Hides
- When God Is Silent
- Where Is Your Faith
- While Men Slept
- Woman! Thou Art Loosed.
- Your Battle And Your Strategy
- Your Foundation And Destiny

- Your Mouth And Your Deliverance
- Your Mouth and Your Warfare

YORUBA PUBLICATIONS
- ADURA AGBAYORI
- ADURA TI NSI OKE NIDI
- OJO ADURA

FRENCH PUBLICATIONS
1. PLUIE DE PRIÈRE
2. ESPIRIT DE VAGABONDAGE
3. EN FINIR AVEC LES FORCES MALÉFIQUES DE LA MAISON DE TON PÉRE
4. QUE l'ENVOUTEMENT PÉRISSE
5. FRAPPEZ l'ADVERSAIRE ET IL FUIRA
6. COMMENT RECEVIOR LA DÉLIVRANCE DU MARI ET DE LA FEMME DE NUIT
7. COMMENT SE DÉLIVRER SOI-MÊME
8. POUVOIR CONTRE LES TERRORITES SPIRITUELS
9. PRIÈRE DE PERCÉES POUR LES HOMMES D'AFFAIRES
10. PRIER JUSQU'À REMPORTER LA VICTOIRE
11. PRIÈRES VIOLENTES POUR HUMILIER LES PROBLÈMES OPINIÂTRES
12. PRIÈRE POUR DÉTRUIRE LES MALADIES ET LES INFIRMITÉS

13. LE COMBAT SPIRITUEL ET LE FOYER
14. BILAN SPIRITUEL PERSONNEL
15. VICTOIRES SUR LES RÊVES SATANIQUES
16. PRIÈRES DE COMBAT CONTRE 70 ESPRITS DÉCHAINÉS
17. LA DÉVIATION SATANIQUE DE LA RACE NOIRE
18. TON COMBAT ET TA STRATÉGIE
19. VOTRE FONDEMENT ET VOTRE DESTIN
20. RÉVOQUER LES DÉCRETS MALÉFIQUES
21. CANTIQUE DES CONTIQUES
22. LE MAUVAIS CRI DES IDOLES
23. QUAND LES CHOSES DEVIENNENT DIFFICILES
24. LES STRATÉGIES DE PRIÈRES POUR LES CÉLIBATAIRES
25. SE LIBÉRER DES ALLIANCES MALÉFIQUES
26. DEMANTELER LA SORCELLERIE
27. LA DÉLIVERANCE: LE FLACON DE MÉDICAMENT DE DIEU
28. LA DÉLIVERANCE DE LA TÊTE
29. COMMANDER LE MATIN
30. NÉ GRAND MAIS LiÉ
31. POUVOIR CONTRE LES DÉMONS TROPICAUX
32. LE PROGRAMME DE TRANFERT DES RICHESSE
33. LES ETUDIANTS A l'ECOLE DE LA PEUR
34. L'ETOILE DANS VOTRE CIEL
35. LES SAISONS DE LA VIE
36. FEMME TU ES LIBEREE

ANNUAL 70 DAYS PRAYER AND FASTING PUBLICATIONS

Prayers That Bring Miracles

Let God Answer By Fire

Prayers To Mount With Wings As Eagles

Prayers That Bring Explosive Increase

Prayers For Open Heavens

Prayers To Make You Fulfil Your Divine Destiny

Prayers That Make God To Answer And Fight By Fire

Prayers That Bring Unchallengeable Victory And Breakthrough Rainfall Bombardments

Prayers That Bring Dominion Prosperity And Uncommon Success

Prayers That Bring Power And Overflowing Progress

Prayers That Bring Laughter And Enlargement Breakthroughs

Prayers That Bring Uncommon Favour And Breakthroughs

Prayers That Bring Unprecedented Greatness & Unmatchable Increase

Prayers That Bring Awesome Testimonies And Turn Around Breakthroughs

about the Book

WHEN YOU NEED A CHANGE

This is a book written for those who desperately stand in need of divine intervention. It is a powerful weapon of change. The chapters are structured to highlight change as an inevitable experience. You will discover that change requires a divine human partnership being put in place. This book will jolt you to consciousness and awaken in your heart a great desire to move forward in life. The prayer points will signal the beginning of a new era.

about the Author

Dr. D. K. Olukoya is the General Overseer of the Mountain of Fire and Miracles Ministries and The Battle Cry Christian Ministries.

The Mountain of Fire and Miracles Ministries' Headquarters is the largest single christian congregation in Africa with attendance of over 120,000 in single meetings.

MFM is a full gospel ministry devoted to the revival of Apostolic signs, Holy Ghost Fireworks, miracles and the unlimited demonstration of the power of God to deliver to the uttermost. Absolute holiness within and without as spiritual insecticide and pre-requisite for heaven is openly taught. MFM is a do-it-yourself Gospel Ministry, where your hands are trained to wage war and your fingers to do battle.

Dr. Olukoya holds a first class honours degree in Micro-biology from the University of Lagos and a PhD in Molecular Genetics from the University of Reading, United Kingdom. As a researcher, he has over seventy scientific publications to his credit.

Anointed by God, Dr. Olukoya is a prophet, evangelist, teacher and preacher of the Word. His life and that of his wife, Shade and their son, Elijah Toluwani are living proofs that all power belongs to God.

978-978-8424-62-8

www.ingramcontent.com/pod-product-compliance
Lightning Source LLC
Chambersburg PA
CBHW061248040426
42444CB00010B/2299